D0532278

IDENTIFYING, UNDERSTANDING AND SOLUTIONS TO

STRESS

MICHAEL COHEN

To my dear parents Loretta and Gerald

Published in 2001 by Caxton Editions
20 Bloomsbury Street
London WC1B 3JH
a member of the Caxton Publishing Group

© copyright 2001 Caxton Publishing Group
Reprint 2002 , 2003
Designed and produced for Caxton Editions
by Open Door Limited

Editing: Mary Morton
Typesetting: Julie Payne
Illustration: Andrew Shepherd, Art Angle
Digital Imagery © copyright 2001 Photodisc, Inc.

All rights reserved. No part of this publication may be reproduced
or transmitted in any form or by any means, electronic or
mechanical, including photocopying, recording or any information
storage and retrieval system, without prior permission in writing
from the copyright owner.

Title: STRESS
ISBN: 1-84067-288-9

IMPORTANT NOTICE
This book is not intended to be a substitute for medical advice or
treatment. Any person with a condition requiring medical attention should
consult a qualified medical practitioner or suitable therapist.

IDENTIFYING, UNDERSTANDING AND SOLUTIONS TO
STRESS

MICHAEL COHEN

CAXTON EDITIONS

CONTENTS

CONTENTS

INTRODUCTION

STRESS – IT'S ON THE INCREASE

Is there anyone that is free of stress in our modern, high-tech world? I doubt it. Too much stress imposes high physical and emotional costs on our lives. There never seems to be enough time and always too much to do. In this new millennium one fact seems certain; stress is on the increase.

Although change can be exciting, it brings with it many conditions that are difficult to cope with. We have always had to deal with work pressures, family problems and the fear of crime and violence, but with the explosion in information technology and communication devices such as email, mobile phones and pagers escaping from it all can seem impossible.

Below: modern-living can be incredibly stressful, with increasing demands on our bodies to do more, in less time.

NOT ALL STRESS IS BAD

Stress in itself is not a bad thing. A certain amount is necessary to motivate you, and without some pressures life would become boring and without purpose. The trick is in learning how to handle stress in a positive and practical way. How you react to stress depends on whether you see yourself in control of a situation or overwhelmed by it.

HOW THIS BOOK CAN HELP

Throughout this book I am going to share with you techniques and strategies I have used with my stressed clients for over 14 years. I have included the methods that proved to be the most successful for the greatest number of people. They are straight-forward, quick to apply and enjoyable. So let us start our journey and begin to turn distress into positive stress.

SO WHAT'S ALL THIS ABOUT STRESS?

Stress is a word that is bandied around a lot these days, usually in the negative sense. Most people view it as something that must be avoided. Relatives, friends and work colleagues may all say that they are under stress. But what is stress? How does it affect you? How do you recognise it?

When a person believes demands made of them exceed their ability to cope they will experience stress.

Right: stress is caused by the inability to cope with the demands made of us.

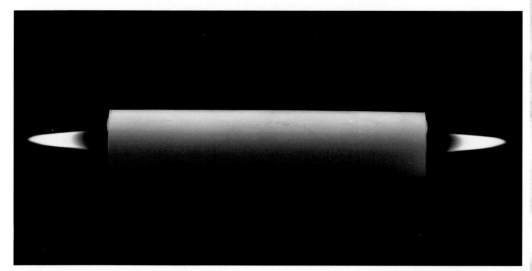

Left: a modern-day representation for stress 'burning the candle at both ends'.

The technical name for these demands is "stressors" and the resulting wear and tear on the body is the stress.

You may think of stress as a relatively new phenomenon; in fact, it has been with us for millions of years. Many years ago when men and women lived in caves life-threatening situations occurred on a daily basis. Cave dwellers hunting for food were regularly exposed to physical dangers from other predators or the environment in which they lived.

Faced with a threat the body reacts immediately – there is a rush of adrenaline, heightened muscle tension, faster heart rate and raised blood pressure. Blood pumps to the muscles and brain causing the body to become alert and as strong as possible for, in order to survive, a hunter would have to respond either by fighting the threat or running away from it. This is called the "fight or flight

response" and is activated whenever a person is faced with an emergency. Physiologist Walter B Cannon first described it over 100 years ago.

The fight or flight response is still experienced by people today and is, of course, appropriate whenever we are faced with a real emergency. However, unlike our ancestors, we are rarely faced with such life-threatening situations. Screaming children, nagging bosses and work deadlines are very unpleasant but hardly life-threatening. The problem is that nature does not know this and will prepare the same fight or flight response. This leaves the body in a high state of arousal which it is unable to utilise.

So if everyday pressures mount up and a person is in this state for long periods of time, their body soon suffers and the experience becomes distress.

Right: everyday we are faced with situations which have the ability to cause us stress; look out for the first stages of stress and be prepared.

THE THREE STAGES OF STRESS

The first scientist to carry out major research on stress was Doctor Hans Selye. Over 50 years ago he described a model of stress which he termed the "General Adaptation Syndrome". According to Dr Selye there are three stages a person will go through when experiencing a stressful event.

STAGE ONE ALARM

During this first stage the person experiences alarm, which immediately triggers a complex cascade of biochemical events and the stress hormones adrenaline and cortisol are pumped into the bloodstream.

STAGE TWO RESISTANCE

In stage two the body's heightened physical responses create an increase in activity so that the person either leaves the situation, or stays and attempts to cope by resisting or adapting to the stressful event.

STAGE THREE EXHAUSTION

By this stage the person has been reacting to the stressful event for so long that they are overwhelmed, their energy is finally depleted and the result is exhaustion. It is then that people become vulnerable to the health problems that are associated with stress. When the alarm bells ring you need to take some action and learn to deal with stress before stress deals with you!

THE SIGNS AND SYMPTOMS OF STRESS

Stress can manifest itself in many different ways, so recognising the signs is an important first step in dealing with your problems. Generally the symptoms will become apparent in five different ways which we describe as emotional, mental, physical, behavioural and health problems. So, without wishing to cause you too much stress, let's takes a look at them.

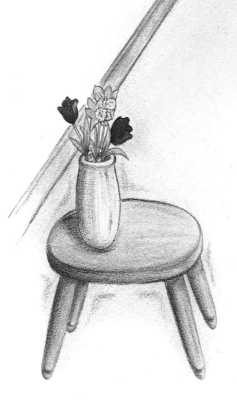

THE EMOTIONAL SYMPTOMS

The emotional symptoms include:
Anxiety.
Nervousness.
Worry.
Depression.
Anger.
Irritability.
Guilt.
Moodiness.
A loss of enjoyment in life.
Loneliness.
Feeling tearful.
Loss of humour.
Lack of confidence.
Isolation.
Dissatisfaction with your job.

THE PHYSICAL SYMPTOMS

The physical symptoms include:

Feeling restless.

Feeling uptight.

Feeling jumpy.

High blood pressure.

Palpitations.

Muscle tensions in the neck and back.

Headaches.

Poor sleep.

Fatigue.

A lack of energy.

Pain.

Dry mouth.

Weakness.

Dizziness.

Trembling.

Grinding of the teeth.

A frequent need to pass water.

Diarrhoea and constipation.

Butterflies in the stomach.

A loss or increase in appetite.

Ringing in the ears.

Cramp.

THE BEHAVIOURAL SYMPTOMS

The behavioural symptoms include:

Impatience.

Impulsiveness.

Hyperactivity.

Short temper.

Aggressiveness.

Becoming accident-prone.

Avoiding difficult situations.

An increase in smoking.

The use of prescribed drugs.

The use of illegal drugs.

Alcohol abuse.

Absenteeism.

Poor work performance.

Loss of sex drive.

Being uncooperative.

Overworking.

Compulsions and obsessions.

Above: The signs and symptoms of stress can affect us in many ways, and the people closest to us.

THE MENTAL SYMPTOMS

The mental symptoms include:

Frequent lapses in memory.
Constant negative thinking.
Being very critical of yourself.
An inability to make decisions.
Difficulty getting things done.
An increase in susceptibility to criticism.
Distorted ideas.
Very rigid attitudes.
Difficulty concentrating.

HEALTH PROBLEMS

Stress is often associated with an increase in physical heath problems including:

High blood pressure.
A higher than usual suscepti-bility to colds and flu.
Migraines.
Irritable bowel syndrome.
Ulcers.
Stomach disorders.
Heart attacks.
Angina.
Strokes.
Asthma.
Skin rashes.

HOW TO ASSESS YOUR STRESS

Read through the list of symptoms and make a note of those that you feel apply to you. Being aware of your symptoms can be a useful sign that stress is on the increase. By working through the book and applying the stress-reducing

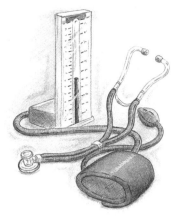

techniques described, you will be able to monitor the reduction in your symptoms.

It is not the purpose of this book to diagnose mental health problems. However, there are some conditions and symptoms that need to be taken seriously. These include depression, anxiety, panic attacks, burnout, and post-traumatic stress disorder.

If you are are experiencing any of the following, for your own peace of mind, consider seeing your doctor:

Depression.
Loss of appetite.
Feel that life is not worth living.
Feel overwhelmed with anxiety.
Loss of energy.
Heart palpitations.

It is also important to seek advice about any physical symptoms such as weight loss, stomach pains and blurred vision.

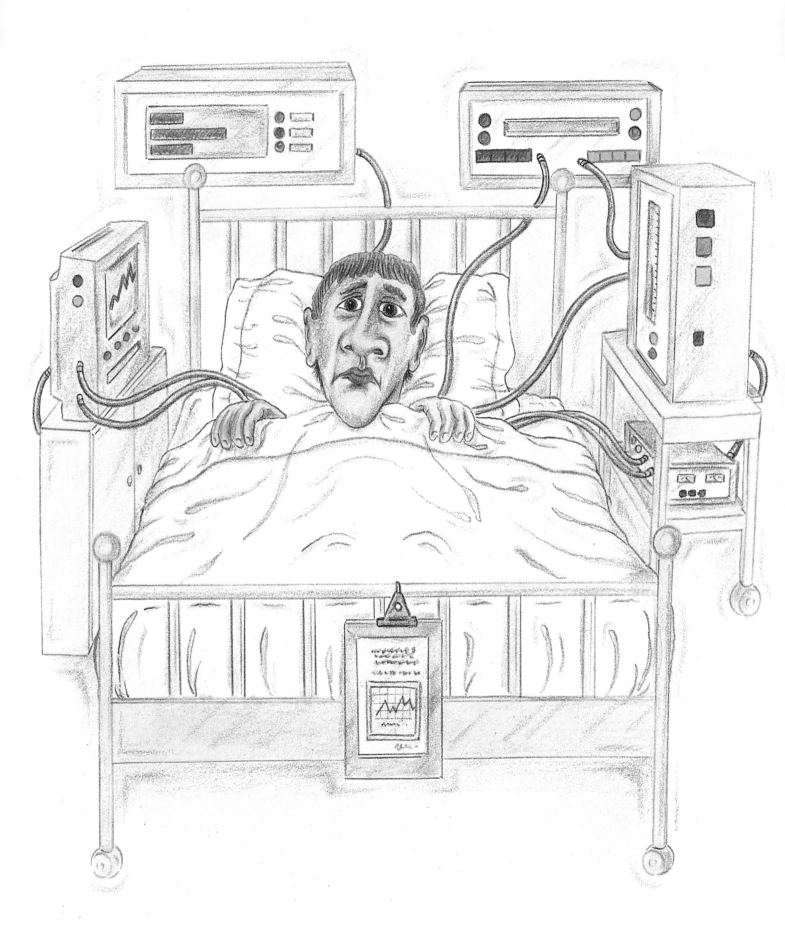

THE STRESS THERMOMETER

One of the most effective ways to measure the amount of stress you are experiencing is to use a "stress thermometer". When you have a fever you take your temperature; it makes sense to do the same for your stress levels. The advantage of the stress thermometer is that it is fast and simple and can be used in virtually any situation.

As you can see from the diagram below zero stands for no stress, 30 means that some stress is being experienced, 50 denotes a moderate amount, 70 is high and finally 100 shows extreme stress.

O　　　　　　　　30　　　　50　　　　70　　　　　　100

LITTLE STRESS　　　MODERATE　　HIGH　　　　EXTREME

Whenever you are experiencing stress, for example, if you are held up in a supermarket queue or have a pile of unfinished paperwork, visualise the thermometer and ask yourself, "How much stress am I experiencing now?" Is it 30, 50 or 100 percent? Once you have started to use the stress-reducing exercises you will be able to take "before" and "after" readings and become familiar with the techniques that are most effective for you in your particular situation.

WHAT IS TRIGGERING YOUR STRESS?
The events and circumstances that trigger stress are many and varied. They are caused by external events (such as noise and traffic) and also by our inner thoughts and attitudes about events. Listed below are some major causes of stress.

Above: work is one of the biggest causes of stress today.

WORK STRESS

It has been suggested that work is the biggest cause of stress in the western world today. The pace of change in the way we work has never been as great. People have to cope with new information technology, longer working hours and short-term contracts. A job is no longer for life. As job insecurity increases, people are more likely to remain in a job that is perhaps safe but not necessarily suited to them.

It is important to examine the sources of stress at work and whenever possible improve your strategies for coping.

FAMILY AND RELATIONSHIP STRESS

People experience high levels of stress in their relationships. From marital conflict and difficult children to alcoholism and violence the problems are wide and varied. These issues need to be properly addressed otherwise the consequences can be serious, leading to separation, divorce and family breakdown.

THE STRESS OF BEREAVEMENT

The loss of a loved one is a devastating life experience. When we lose someone close, it is natural to go through a process of mourning. The emotions and stages of the grieving process will vary from person to person. First there is the initial shock of the loss and at this time it is common to experience a feeling of numbness. Anger, guilt, and despair follow as the reality of the loss deepens. This is followed by recovery as the person accepts the bereavement and begins to rebuild their life. It is important to acknowledge the grief and talk to someone close.

THE STRESS OF FINANCIAL PROBLEMS

Financial problems obviously cause an enormous amount of stress. The loss of a job, an addiction to gambling or mounting bills can lead to family tensions. Ignoring the problem will only make matters worse. When faced with money worries, it is important not to panic. Instead talk to your debtors and set a realistic budget.

THE STRESS OF CHANGE

Changes in your life, however big or small, whether positive or negative, can create stress. Major life changes such as starting a new job, getting married or moving house can challenge our abilities to cope. This is particularly true if we experience too many changes in a short period of time. Although change is an inevitable part of life, it makes sense to plan ahead. 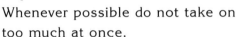 Whenever possible do not take on too much at once.

ENVIRONMENTAL STRESS

Our environment is a big factor in the cause of stress. We have to contend with crowded trains, noisy traffic and polluted cities. These conditions can lead to health-related problems such as asthma, allergies and migraine headaches. We cannot easily escape the environment we live in. However, healthy eating, exercise and regular breaks can help us to better cope with the stresses and strains of city life.

Although I have listed some of the major triggers of stress, you may want to think about other causes that are are specific to you.

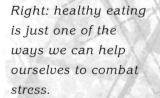

Right: healthy eating is just one of the ways we can help ourselves to combat stress.

HOW YOUR THINKING AFFECTS YOUR STRESS

YOUR ATTITUDE COUNTS

As we have seen from the triggers listed previously, external events do play a part in the stress we experience. However, it is important to take into consideration our attitude towards these events.

The way we think about a situation can have a direct bearing on the amount of stress we experience.

Let us consider the common experience of being stuck in traffic. As we observe the different drivers in their cars we may notice many of them getting very worked up. Some are sounding their car horns and even shouting at the traffic, as if that would magically move it on. Others remain calm taking the time to listen to some music or chat to their passengers.

This is an example of people reacting to the same event in opposite ways with different emotions and behaviours. The drivers who become upset are reacting to the experience of the traffic hold-up in a way that is certain to cause distress. It is a fact that our negative thinking causes a large part of the stress we experience.

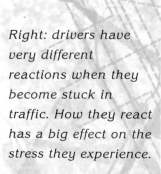

Right: drivers have very different reactions when they become stuck in traffic. How they react has a big effect on the stress they experience.

Imagine that you are on your way to an important meeting and are lost. In a hurry, you call to someone on the opposite side of the road to ask for directions. They fail to answer you. In a louder voice and with your emotions rising, you ask again – still no reply. Now feeling angry, you tell him to forget it and continue on your way. While looking for someone else to ask, you think to yourself, "If I had more time I would give that man a piece of my mind."

Later on you are having lunch in the restaurant where the meeting is being held. There is a tap on your shoulder. As you turn around, you see the man who ignored you earlier in the day. He apologises for seeming to ignore you but explains that he is hard of hearing. What happens to your anger now? Do you still consider him to be rude? Now you have more time, are you still going to give him a piece of your mind? The likelihood is that your feelings would probably change. Instead of anger you might feel embarrassment, possibly even guilt. From this example it can be seen that people can have different feelings about a situation when they view it from a different perspective.

Let us think back to the traffic jam example. You will remember that some drivers became very angry, sounding their car horns and shouting at the traffic. Most people

would conclude that the reason for their anger was due to being stuck in the traffic. To a large extent this makes sense; there are not many people who like being kept waiting. However, this fails to explain why other drivers faced with exactly the same situation remained calm.

Below: being late for an appointment or becoming lost on the way, causes stress which gives you a different perspective on the events which happen around you.

To explain the differences in the drivers' attitudes and reactions we are going to look at a model of emotional upset first described by the American psychologist Dr Albert Ellis, the pioneer of Rational Emotive Behaviour Therapy. He calls this the ABC model. A is known as the activating event, meaning any potentially stressful situation. B stands for beliefs, a person's thoughts and attitudes about A. Finally C stands for the consequence meaning a person's feelings and actions.

A Event
The potentially stressful situation.

B Beliefs
A person's thoughts and attitudes about A.

C Consequence
A person's feelings and actions.

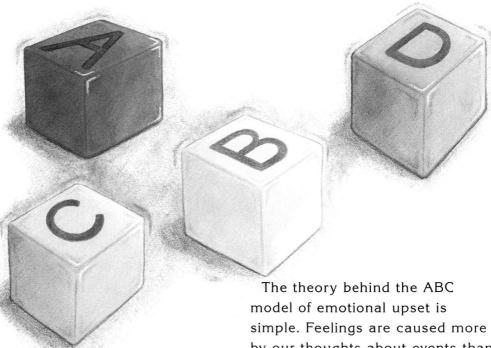

The theory behind the ABC model of emotional upset is simple. Feelings are caused more by our thoughts about events than by the events themselves. According to the ABC model, it was not being stuck in the traffic jam that was responsible for the drivers' different feelings, but the way they were thinking about the situation.

Left: being stuck in traffic is becoming a daily routine for many people in the modern world, therefore, coping with the stress it causes is extremely important.

A driver remaining calm was probably thinking:

*This is a nuisance but not the end of the world.
There is not a lot I can do so I shall have to grin and bear it.
I might as well sit back and make the best of things.*

A	**Event** Driver stuck in traffic.
B	**Beliefs** *This traffic must move right now.* *It is just awful.* *I can't stand it any longer.*
C	**Consequence** Anger. Shouting at the traffic and sounding car horn.

A driver getting angry was probably thinking:

This traffic must move right now. It is just awful. I can't stand it any longer.

In the ABC format it looks like this (below left).

The above beliefs are an example of what Dr Albert Ellis has called irrational thinking and would lead anyone who thought in this way to become angry. Many people would question the idea that the above set of beliefs could be called irrational. Given the circumstances of being stuck in traffic, wouldn't anyone think in this way? This is a good question; in order to answer it we need to take a close look at the make up of irrational thinking.

WHAT MAKES THINKING IRRATIONAL?

The characteristics of irrational beliefs are:

They are unrealistic.
They are rigid.
They blow events way out of proportion.
They lead to unhealthy feelings that cause distress.
When a person is holding an irrational belief they are demanding that events and circumstances be different from the way they actually are by using words such as "must" and "should".

e.g. I must do well.
You should treat me well.
Life must go the way I demand.

It is not the words in themselves, but the attitude behind the words that cause the problem.

Below: irrational thoughts lead to feeling stressed about any given situation.

People can also exaggerate the badness of events by using such words as "awful" and "terrible".

e.g. It's awful.
It's terrible.
I can't stand it.

Whenever a person thinks in this unhelpful way they will experience emotional pain such as anger, anxiety, guilt and depression. This inevitably will lead to distress.

In the traffic jam example the driver is holding the rigid belief "The traffic must move now". In reality will demanding that the traffic *must* move now help to move it on? Secondly he is exaggerating the badness of the event by describing it as awful. It is certainly annoying to be held up in traffic but can it truly be described as awful? Finally, why can't he stand it? In reality people can stand almost anything.

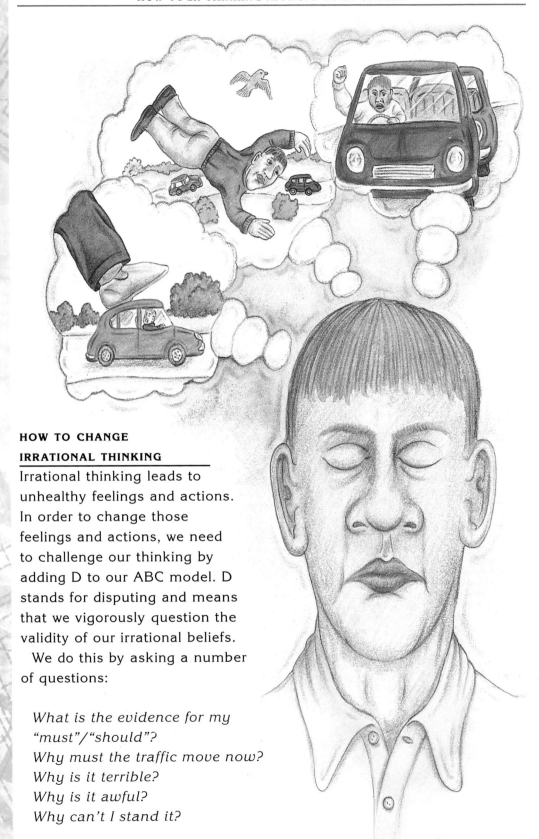

HOW TO CHANGE IRRATIONAL THINKING

Irrational thinking leads to unhealthy feelings and actions. In order to change those feelings and actions, we need to challenge our thinking by adding D to our ABC model. D stands for disputing and means that we vigorously question the validity of our irrational beliefs.

We do this by asking a number of questions:

What is the evidence for my "must"/"should"?
Why must the traffic move now?
Why is it terrible?
Why is it awful?
Why can't I stand it?

The following example will illustrate how to challenge irrational beliefs.

Jenny is a secretary who recently lost her job at an advertising company. When she came to see me for counselling she was feeling depressed and felt it was not worth looking for new employment.

At B, Jenny was thinking

I should not have lost my job.
I can't stand it.
I am totally incompetent.
I will never get another job like that one again.

A   **Event**
Jenny loses her job.

B   **Beliefs**
I should not have lost my job.
I can't stand it.
I am totally incompetent.
I will never get another job like that one again.

C   **Consequence**
Feeling depressed and unable to look for a new job.

Left: irrational beliefs must be challenged and conquered in order to relieve stress.

After Jenny talked the situation though with me, she was able to see that her depression had more to do with her irrational thinking than the job loss itself. In particular she was doing a first-class job at running herself down. Once she was aware of this, Jenny was ready to challenge her irrational beliefs. This is how she did it.

D. Why should I have not lost my job?

Although I would have strongly preferred not to have lost my job, there is no law that states I should not have lost it.

D. Why can't I stand losing my job?

Well in reality I can stand losing my job. I have faced difficult situations before and coped. I can cope with this one, too.

D. What evidence exists that I am totally incompetent?

No evidence exists for this idea. I have made a number of mistakes at this job but that doesn't prove that I am totally flawed – just human. I have done well in past jobs and I can do well again.

D. What evidence exists that I will never get another job?

There is no evidence; I am a competent woman with a lot of skills and work experience to offer. I have found other jobs before and I can do so again.

Far left: freeing your mind of irrational thoughts leaves it open to positive thinking.

RATIONAL BELIEFS

The characteristics of rational beliefs are:

They are realistic.
They are flexible.
They do not blow events out of proportion.
They lead to healthy appropriate feelings.

Challenging irrational beliefs helps a person to form rational beliefs and change the way they feel about an event. By disputing her ideas about the job loss, Jenny was able to change her demand that she should not have lost her job into a healthy preference for not losing it. Being unemployed was a setback but, by reminding herself that she had a lot of skills to offer, Jenny was able to see that the situation was not awful. She had been in similar situations before and she could find another job again. Jenny was now ready to add E, which stands for Effective new thinking. It looked like this.

Although I would have strongly preferred not to have lost my job, I did. I have faced difficult situations before and coped. I can cope again. I have made a number of mistakes at this job but that does not make me flawed – just human. I have done well in the past and I can do well again.

After changing her thinking, Jenny felt sad but no longer depressed. To feel sadness after a job loss is healthy. It would be unrealistic to expect her to feel over the moon given the circumstances. Depression on the other hand is an unhealthy emotion and is often an indication that a person is thinking in an irrational way.

SELF-HELP FORM

A useful way to reduce your distress is to use a self-help form to identify, challenge and then change your irrational thinking. The first thing to do when you are feeling distress is to stop what you are doing and take a reading with your stress thermometer. Then take three slow deep breaths, get a sheet of paper and a pen and at the top of the page write:

A. The event

Here you describe the situation. Try and be specific.

B. Irrational beliefs

Identify and write down your irrational beliefs about the event. Remember, irrational beliefs are rigid and contain words such as "should" and "must", e.g. "things must go the way I demand". They exaggerate the badness of an event,

Right: when you become distressed, take time out and use a self help form to identify, challenge and then change your rational thinking.

turning a nuisance into a horror: "It's awful/terrible. I can't stand it."

C. Consequences
Write down how you felt and acted in relation to the event.

D. Disputing
Vigorously question the validity of your irrational beliefs by asking the questions contained on page 31.

E. Effective new thinking
Write down your new rational beliefs.

F. New feelings and actions
Write down how you now feel and act.

Take another reading with the stress thermometer and feel the difference.

Above: resolving a problem amicably will reduce the risk of long-term stress in a business situation. A self-help form can help you do this successfully.

Jim, a 40-year-old businessman, consulted me because of work stress. One particular stress trigger was his business partner David's quirky sense of humour. At meetings with clients or staff David would frequently make wisecracks. This would anger Jim and often led to disagreement and arguments. Jim told me that over the past two years he had tried a number of strategies to try and get David to express himself in a different manner. This had led nowhere.

He stated that he wanted to look at more effective ways of communicating the problem to David and see if that might improve matters. I agreed that this was a good idea but thought that we should first help Jim reduce his anger about David's behaviour. Jim could see that by remaining calm he would be in a better frame of mind to talk the problem through with David.

Here is an example of how Jim used a self-help form:

A. The event

A meeting with clients in which David's presentation is full of wisecracks.

B. Irrational beliefs

David must be more serious.
He is an irresponsible and awful person.
I can't stand his wisecracks.

C. Consequences

Anger that led to an argument

D. Disputing

Why must David be more serious?
There is no law that states that he must be more serious.
However I would strongly prefer that he was.

What evidence exists that he is irresponsible and an awful person?
None. He might have a peculiar sense of humour, but that does not make him irresponsible.

Why can't I stand his wisecracking manner?
Actually I have stood it for the past two years. It's a nuisance but hardly life-threatening.

E. Effective new thinking

I would prefer that David addressed meetings without all these wisecracks but he doesn't have to.
He might have a strange way of expressing himself but that hardly makes him an irresponsible person. It's a nuisance that he conducts himself at meetings in this way – but I can stand it.

F. New feelings and actions

Feeling mildly annoyed, but not as angry. Believe I can talk to him about the problem in a constructive way.

Before Jim filled in the self-help form his stress thermometer felt as high as 70, afterwards it felt more like 50, which was a moderate improvement. However, by repeating his effective new thinking silently several times during the day he reduced it to 30 – a big improvement.

Above: with effort and practice even long-term irrational thinkers can learn how to control their thoughts and emotions.

You may be thinking; is it really that easy? Do I only have to identify and change my irrational thinking in order to reduce my stress? The process of filling in a self-help form is indeed quite easy. With some practice you will soon get the hang of it. Changing the way you feel will take a little longer and to quote Dr Ellis requires "Work and practice".

You may have to go over your new thinking several times like Jim did. Take into account that when under stress most people have difficulty thinking rationally. You have probably been thinking in irrational ways for a long time. However, with effort and practice, you will soon find yourself getting less upset.

RELAX WITH EASE

Many people make the mistake of thinking that they do not have the time to relax. Others believe that relaxation is only for winding down at the end of a hard day. One of my clients believed that time spent following a relaxation procedure would impede his efficiency at work, but after a few weeks' practice he felt more alert and better able to concentrate. Waiting for a stressful event to occur is not the best time to begin learning relaxation. It is far better to set aside 20 minutes a day for practice. Once you have learnt it, you will be able to let go of your tension in virtually any situation.

Relaxation produces a wonderful feeling of wellbeing, helping to relax tense muscles.

It can also:

Reduce your anxiety.
Eliminate fatigue.
Improve physical and mental performance.
Help you to get to sleep.
Manage pain.
Lower your blood pressure.
Manage irritable bowel syndrome.

RELAXATION

PROGRESSIVE RELAXATION

Progressive relaxation is a technique that focuses on deep muscle relaxation. It was first developed in the 1920s by Dr Edmund Jacobson and over the years has been refined and modified This technique involves tightening different muscle groups. If you have neck or back problems, you may wish to modify the procedure. Never practise while driving or when your concentration is needed elsewhere.

The procedure is as follows:

1 Sit or lie down in a quiet comfortable place. Remove contact lenses and any sharp objects such as jewellery. Uncross your arms and legs. Take in a deep breath and hold for as long as you find it comfortable. Breathe out – letting all feelings of tension leave your body.

2 Clench your right fist, tighter and tighter. Notice the tension in your clenched fist, hand and arm. Now relax your fist and feel your right hand and arm go loose and limp. Notice the contrast with the tension. Repeat the procedure with your left fist and then with both fists.

3 Focus your attention on your forehead. Pull your eyebrows together as tightly as possible and hold. Now relax and let your forehead smooth out. Notice the contrast between tension and relaxation. Repeat the procedure and notice how relaxed your forehead can become.

4 Close your eyes together as tightly as possible, feeling the tension. Now relax your eyes, letting your eyelids droop. Keeping your eyes closed, repeat the procedure. Let your eyes remain closed for the rest of the exercise.

5 Clench your jaw biting your back teeth together. Feel the tension as it spreads throughout your jaw. Now relax your jaw. Once again, notice the contrast between tension and relaxation, then repeat the procedure.

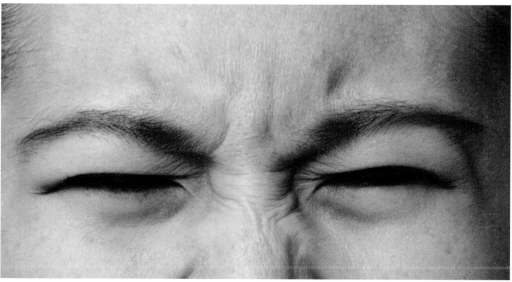

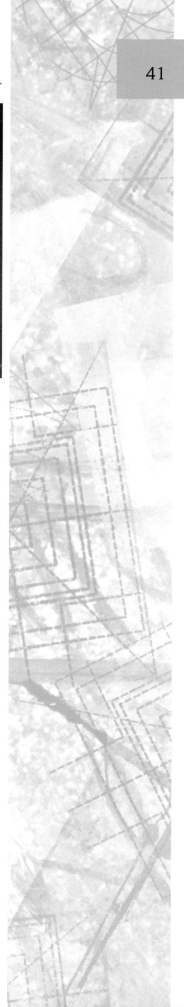

6 Pull your head back as far as is comfortable. Feel the tension in your neck, hold and then roll your head slowly to the right and then to the left. Notice the tension. Then straighten your head and bring it forward, pushing your chin onto your chest. Feel the tension in the back of your neck. Relax and allow your head to return to a comfortable position. Repeat the procedure and allow the relaxation to deepen.

7 Hunch your shoulders and hold for as long as is comfortable. Feel the tension. Then let your shoulders relax. Feel the relaxation spreading. Repeat the procedure and see how relaxed your shoulders can become.

8 Focus on the rhythm of your breathing, the rising and the falling of your diaphragm and chest. Notice how heavy your body is becoming. With every breath that you take, feel your body relax just that little bit more.

9 Pull in your stomach muscles. Hold for as long as is comfortable, feel the tension and then relax. Repeat the procedure.

10 Tighten your buttocks and thighs. Push your heels down as hard as you can. Feel the tension. Hold for as long as is comfortable and then relax. Notice the contrast between the tension and relaxation. Then repeat the procedure.

11 Point your toes in a downward direction and notice your calves getting tense. Feel the tension and hold for as long as is comfortable. Then relax. Repeat the procedure.

Focus your attention on the comfortable feelings in your body. From the top of your head to the tips of your toes, notice how relaxed you have become. You can now drift off to a relaxing place in your imagination. It can be somewhere familiar to you. Or it may be an imaginary place that only exists in your mind. When you are ready open your eyes.

For best results practise progressive relaxation on a daily basis for approximately 20 minutes.

It is important to take your time and not rush through the technique. After practising the procedure, you may notice tension in parts of your body that you thought did not exist. This is not an unusual experience and is an indication that you are becoming aware of the parts of your body where you hold on to tension. With practice this will pass.

You may find it beneficial to make a tape recording of the procedure or have someone talk you through it.

Left: when relaxing drift off to a place in your imagination. It can be somewhere familiar to you. Or it may be an imaginary place that only exists in your mind.

THE BRIEF RELAXATION TECHNIQUE

You can benefit from learning a brief method of relaxation. This is especially helpful if you find yourself in a stressful situation that requires you to let go of tension immediately. For example, Lisa – who was studying for her degree in economics – came to see me because she was behind in her studies and under immense stress. Lisa told me that the harder she tried to study, the more stress and anxiety she would experience. She was convinced that she would fail her exams.

I spent some time with Lisa looking at how she approached her studies and how her irrational thinking might be contributing towards her distress. I suggested to her that she take regular breaks from her studies and practise the brief relaxation technique. She found this very helpful and reported that it reduced her anxiety and improved her concentration.

You can also practise this technique for a couple of minutes every two to three hours to keep distress at bay. All you need to do is:

1. Sit in a comfortable chair.

2. Relax and close your eyes.

3. Focus on the rhythm of your breathing.

4. Let your whole body become loose and limp.

5. Imagine a relaxing scene. Many of my clients find this simple process helpful in stressful working environments where taking regular breaks can sometimes prove difficult. This is equally true if you are a homemaker with demanding young children to take care of.

Left: when practising your relaxation technique try to visualise a relaxing scene such as a sunset or a field of corn swaying in the wind.

PICTURE YOUR STRESS AWAY

You can use your mind to help you relax by creating pleasant images in your imagination.

This is called visualisation and can involve all of your senses. For example, if you were to imagine yourself on a beach you could picture the sand, feel the warmth of the sun, hear the sound of the sea and smell the salt air.

Imagery can also be used to create and recreate emotions. For instance, you could imagine a past experience when you felt very calm and relaxed.

Tom, another client of mine, told me how he used the power of visualisation to create his own imaginary safe place. Whenever he felt that stress was getting the better of him, he would go to this place to "recharge his emotional battery". After going to his safe place for five minutes he felt revitalised.

This is how it is done:

1. Sit in a comfortable chair and close your eyes.

3. Focus on the rhythm of your breathing.

4. In your mind create a picture of a comfortable relaxing place.

5. Allow yourself to feel relaxed and safe in this place. Think of it as somewhere where you can just be yourself and let go of all your troubles.

6. When you are ready open your eyes.

You can go to your safe place whenever you feel the need. You can use it as a place to resolve problems, to think things through or to just switch off. The more you practise, the easier it will become.

Far left: use your mind to help you relax by creating pleasant images in your imagination.

BREATHE YOUR STRESS AWAY

When we feel under threat, our breathing rate increases in preparation for fight or flight, but if this response is inappropriate we can feel anxious and short of breath.

In order to achieve a good quality of relaxation, you need to learn how to breathe correctly. This may surprise you; after all you have been breathing since you were born. Many people who experience stress and anxiety are breathing in a shallow way from their chest. People who are relaxed are breathing slowly and deeply from their abdomen. One of the most effective ways of switching off stress and anxiety is to practise deep breathing.

Here is the process:

1. Sit down in a comfortable place.

2. Tune into the rhythm of your breathing.

3. Put your hand on your stomach. As you breathe, try and feel your stomach moving up and down. The aim is to breathe from your stomach instead of from your chest.

4. When this has been achieved slow the rate of your breathing down.

At first you may find it difficult to breathe from your stomach. To get a comfortable rhythm you may find it helpful to say the word *relax* as you breathe out. One of my clients would imagine all her stress leaving in a black cloud. As you keep practising, you will find your body becoming more relaxed.

SCAN YOUR STRESS AWAY

A fast and effective way to check for stress is to use a technique called scanning. The idea is to mentally scan through your body from the top of your head to the tips of your toes to discover where you are holding tension. Whether you are driving to work or waiting at a supermarket checkout, scanning is easy to practise. The basic idea is to direct your attention throughout your body, find your tension then let it go.

This is how it is done:

1. Spend a few moments focusing on the rhythm of your breathing.

2. Breathe in and mentally scan an area of your body for tension.

3. Breathe out, relaxing the tense area.

4. Move on to the next area of your body repeating the process.

Scan your body at regular intervals throughout the day. You can remind yourself to do this by putting notes in your diary or around your home.

Left: take the time to scan your stress away.

Right: Self-hypnosis is a straightforward, effective and non-mystical way of relaxing the mind and body which can be practised virtually anywhere that you are able to relax.

RELAX WITH SELF-HYPNOSIS

Self-hypnosis is a straightforward, effective and non-mystical way of relaxing the mind and body. In a deeply relaxed state, you can repeat to yourself autosuggestions such as "I will feel calm and relaxed" in situations where you would normally feel distress.

Self–hypnosis involves the following:

1. Make yourself comfortable, sitting or lying down.

2. Without moving your head, slowly roll your eyes up as high as you can.

3. Take a slow, deep abdominal breath, hold momentarily and, as you exhale, close your eyes relaxing the muscles around the eyes.

4. Continue to breathe slowly and naturally as you allow the relaxed feeling to spread from the top of your head all the way down to the tips of your toes, letting go of any feelings of physical tension.

5. To deepen this state of relaxation, count backwards from 5 down to 1, counting on each inhalation, and, as you exhale, mentally repeat a word such as

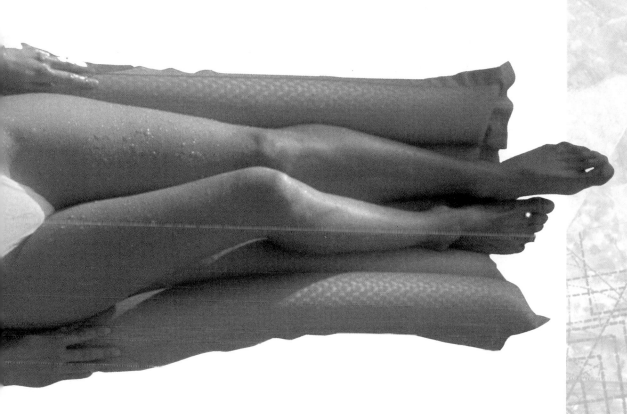

"relax" or "peace" or another word that has meaning for you.

6. When you feel completely relaxed, give yourself auto-suggestions such as "I can remain calm and relaxed in this situation".

7. End the self-hypnosis by counting up from 1 to 5, opening your eyes at the count of five.

When working with self-hypnosis, it is important to keep your autosuggestions realistic and positive. Refrain from using suggestions such as "I will try and relax" or "I must relax". The first implies a struggle

and the second is a demand that may lead to more stress. Practise self-hypnosis unhurriedly two to three times a day. The whole self–hypnosis exercise will take about five minutes to practise.

All of the above relaxation techniques can help reduce distress. Unlike alcohol and drugs, their only side effects are an increased feeling of well-being. However, the techniques become more effective if you also work at changing your irrational thoughts. Keep practising and build on each success. Persevere and, above all, do not be put off by setbacks.

EMOTIONS AND DISTRESS

Let us face facts: feelings cause distress. Emotions such as anger, anxiety and depression can paralyse, blocking us from achieving our goals. As previously explained, we have far more control over our emotions than we might think. So let us now take a closer look at how to manage emotions that lead to distress.

Rightt: try to channel your anger in a creative way and turn it into a positive force instead of a negative.

ANGER

Anger is one of the most destructive emotions we can experience. When someone or something does not live up to our expectations, we feel anger because we may hold the following types of beliefs:

You must treat me the way I want.
You are a terrible person.
Life must be fair.

The problem with this attitude is that, however hard we might try, we cannot control other people or the world.

Anger can have a detrimental effect on physical and emotional health. It is often a signal that something needs to be dealt with and if left unchecked, anger can lead to violence. Therapists sometimes teach their clients to express their anger in a physical way by hitting cushions or screaming out. Sometimes, however, this can have the effect of strengthening the angry feelings, so it is far better to change your irrational beliefs and then try and resolve the matter in a practical way.

HOW TO COPE WITH ANGER

Recognise that anger is a natural human emotion that is not bad or evil. It is what you do with your anger that matters.

Learn to recognise the situations and circumstances that lead to your anger so that you can be better prepared for them.

Remember that it is not events in themselves, but our view about events that causes feelings such as anger. Whenever you can, challenge your irrational beliefs.

Practise relaxation techniques and use them whenever your anger is triggered. Deep breathing can be especially helpful for this.

If you become angry with someone, take a deep breath, silently count to 10, then if appropriate talk the matter through in an assertive, non-aggressive way.

See if you can look at the situation from a different perspective. Ask yourself "Is this really worth getting so angry about?" You may even be able to laugh at the situation.

Channel your anger in a creative way: writing, drawing, art, music, and exercise – all these mediums can turn anger into a positive force.

ANGER MANAGEMENT THROUGH VISUALISATION

Peter was angry. It was his third visit to the store and his computer had still not been repaired. To make matters worse, the manager could not confirm exactly when the computer would be ready. Peter became aggressive, shouting at the top of his voice. After the manager threatened to call the police, Peter left the store in disgust.

Now this aggressive behaviour was not an isolated incident and Peter wanted to learn how to control it. I introduced Peter to a visualisation method where he pictured himself remaining calm in trying circumstances.

The following rehearsal method helped Peter to reduce his anger:

1. Sit in a comfortable position, close your eyes, breathe slowly/ calmly and relax.

2. Vividly imagine a situation in which you become angry. See and hear yourself as you build up your feelings of anger. Observe your posture, feel your tension. Notice how the other person responds to your behaviour.

3. Once you can really feel your anger, silently repeat a coping phrase to yourself such as "I can remain calm", "It's not worth getting angry", "Why let him/her push my buttons?", "I can choose not to get angry", "Just because he/she has made an unpleasant remark does not mean I have to agree with it".

Repeat the process until you feel a reduction in your anger.

The idea is to reduce your angry feelings and behaviour but not to imagine the other person responding differently. We can learn to control our own attitudes but not other people's.

However, when you learn to manage your behaviour better you may notice others changing too.

ANGER IN RELATIONSHIPS

Disagreements, though painful, are a natural part of most couples' relationships. However, blazing arguments can get completely out of hand with accusations and threats flying.

Instead of clearing the air, this behaviour can leave couples feeling hurt and angry and stop them talking to each other for days. Good communication is an effective way of reducing arguments and one of the most important elements of a satisfying and long-lasting relationship.

Left: Disagreements are a natural part of most couples' relationships but it is essential to keep these under control.

THE ELEMENTS OF EFFECTIVE COMMUNICATION

Below I describe some of the most common mistakes that lead to arguments and some examples to change your style of communication.

Attacking

This is when your partner may say, "You just don't understand" and you fail to acknowledge their feelings and go on to attack and criticise.

Hint: Even if you think what they are saying is wrong, the key is to acknowledge that this is how they are feeling. Empathising in this way will have the effect of lowering the temperature because your partner will feel you are making an attempt to understand their feelings. You can then go on to express how you feel.

Over-generalising

"You are totally selfish" is an example of an over-generalisation. It implies that a person is selfish 100 percent of the time. But do occasional acts of selfishness make a person totally selfish?

Hint: When communicating, try and make your comments as specific as possible, e.g. "I think you acted in a selfish way when you refused to give Angela a lift home".

Far right: good communication is essential in a good relationship.

Criticising

There are two forms of criticism. The first type is negative and consists of putdowns such as: "You always do this", "You never do that". The second form of criticism is constructive. It requests that a person change their behaviour.

Hint: Make your criticisms constructive by asking for a specific change. It is unhelpful to say, "You never close the garage door". Instead, try saying, "In the future can you please remember to close the garage door".

Denying

You tell your partner that you do not feel hurt and angry when in reality you do. You deny your true feelings because you fear dire consequences if you speak up. You could be thinking, "If I speak up for myself he will be furious and leave me."

Hint: Imagining disasters will often hold you back from self-expression and, like the swing of a pendulum, can lead to future aggressive outbursts. Effective communication includes assertiveness, which means letting your partner know, in a non-threatening way, that you do not like something they are doing, have done or said.

Bad timing

You have had a difficult day, you are hungry and your partner wants to talk. Not exactly a good time for constructive communication.

Hint: Tell your partner that it is important to talk things over – but not at this precise moment. Ask for half an hour's "time out" so you can relax and then you will be happy to talk.

You can practise being assertive in front of a mirror, in your imagination and by recording your new communication style on a cassette tape. Good communication is a skill that takes practice. You will get it wrong sometimes – but that is because you are human. With practice, you will succeed.

Far right: felling depressed can seriously affect a person's ability to function, both physically and mentally.

DEPRESSION

Clinical depression is one of the most painful mood states that can be experienced. There is a vast difference between feeling down in the dumps and depressed. The symptoms can be both physical and emotional and seriously affect a person's ability to function. Depression has often been described as anger turned inward. This is often the result of people blaming themselves for not living up to their own expectations or the expectations they believe others have of them.

People commonly think of depression as a sign of weakness and label themselves as useless. It can be especially painful to be told "Pull yourself together" – because that is exactly what the depressed person wishes they could do. The fact is that clinical depression is a serious condition that requires medical and psychological evaluation.

The symptoms of depression include:

Feelings of hopelessness.
Lack of motivation.
Low self-esteem.
Feeling guilty.
Negative thinking.
Suicidal thoughts and feelings.
Sleep disturbance.
Appetite or weight changes.
Loss of sex drive.
Loss of interest in life.
Fatigue.

HOW TO COPE WITH DEPRESSION

Identify what may have caused your depression. It is important to identify what may have triggered your depression. Have you recently suffered a loss? Moved home? Are you isolated from your family and friends? Do you think of yourself as a failure? Once you have identified the possible reasons for your depression, you will be in a better position to do something about it.

1. Exercise on a regular basis

Swimming, walking or riding a bicycle are all good forms of exercise and will release endorphins, the body's natural anti-depressant hormone.

2. Put some structure into your day

Include activities that you would normally find pleasurable. You may think that in order to achieve something you have to feel like doing it. In fact the reverse is often true; it is the doing that will give you the feeling of accomplishment and will spur you on to achieve your goals.

3. Talk to someone you trust

When you are feeling depressed communication is important. Express how you feel by talking to friends and members of your family.

4. Challenge your negative thinking

You may have noticed that when you feel depressed your style of thinking is pessimistic. You may have thoughts such as "I shouldn't be feeling like this" or "I am a weak person for feeling depressed". Identify your irrational thinking and challenge it. Stop defining yourself as incompetent and useless.

5. Seek professional help

Sometimes depression is the result of a chemical imbalance and may need to be treated by medication. Counselling and psychotherapy can be helpful for most types of depression. Whatever the cause of your depression, it is important to seek professional help.

6. The distortions in your thinking

The psychiatrists Aaron Beck, who developed cognitive therapy, and David Burns, an innovator in the field, have identified specific forms of distorted thinking. Called cognitive distortions, they can lead to feelings of depression and other negative emotions. Some of the most common types of cognitive distortions are:

7. All or nothing thinking

This involves looking at things as either black or white, good or bad, leaving no room for middle ground. You might believe "Either I succeed at everything I attempt or else I am a total failure".

Far left: exercise on a regular basis, even if it is just walking the dog, will release endorphins to help combat depression.

Jim had successfully stopped smoking for three months but then experienced a stressful event resulting in him smoking one cigarette. Jim thought, "That's it, I've blown it completely!" This thought upset him so much that he went on to smoke an entire packet of cigarettes.

8. Predicting the future

Without evidence, you predict that things will turn out badly. After being ill for three months Penny thought, "I will never have the energy to work again". Happily Penny returned to work the following month. Whenever Penny starts to worry she now asks herself, "Am I jumping to conclusions?"

9. Mind reading

Again without evidence, you believe you know what other people think about you. At a social gathering Sandra accidentally dropped a glass of wine. She thought to herself, "People will think of me as totally incompetent". Moments later someone she had never met told Sandra that only the previous week she had dropped a drink in a similar situation. That was the start of a new friendship.

10. Labelling

When you have done something wrong or made a mistake you label yourself a "failure", "stupid", "weak" etc. When Richard failed to complete his exam paper, he thought, "I'm a failure". Labelling is irrational because you are not the same as what you do. You are therefore not a failure but a human being that will sometimes fail.

11. Mental filter

You filter out all the positive aspects of a situation and focus only on the negative details. Despite four newspapers giving excellent reviews of Michael's performance in an amateur play, one paper was mildly critical. Michael ignored all the positive feedback and focused exclusively on the negative review. When people focus exclusively on the negative they greatly reduce their happiness.

12. Personalisation

When something bad happens, you may see it as totally your fault. Even though you may have little if anything to do with the situation, you blame yourself and overlook how others might be involved. Patrick's 13-year-old son was caught stealing sweets from a shop. Even though Patrick had always tried to teach his son right from wrong he thought, "This proves what a poor role model I am".

HOW TO LIFT YOURSELF OUT OF DEPRESSION

Dr David Burns has suggested a powerful way of transforming your mood.

This is how it is done:

Take a pen and paper and draw a line down the middle of the page.

In the left-hand column, write down all of your negative thoughts about an upsetting situation.

Look at each thought and begin to challenge them by asking yourself the following questions.

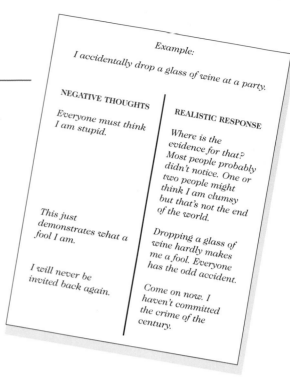

Example:
I accidentally drop a glass of wine at a party.

NEGATIVE THOUGHTS	REALISTIC RESPONSE
Everyone must think I am stupid.	*Where is the evidence for that? Most people probably didn't notice. One or two people might think I am clumsy but that's not the end of the world.*
This just demonstrates what a fool I am.	*Dropping a glass of wine hardly makes me a fool. Everyone has the odd accident.*
I will never be invited back again.	*Come on now. I haven't committed the crime of the century.*

What errors am I making in my thinking?
Am I looking at things as either black or white, leaving no room for middle ground?
Am I predicting the future, thinking that things will turn out badly without the evidence to support my conclusions?
Am I mind reading, believing that people are thinking badly of me without evidence to back it up?
Am I labelling myself?
Am I focusing exclusively on the negative and ignoring the positive?
Am I personalising – seeing the situation as totally my fault?

In the right-hand column, substitute more realistic thoughts that counteract the negative ones.

This straightforward technique is a very helpful way of changing your feelings and lifting you out of a depressed state.

Right: take steps to lift yourself out of your depression and transform your mood into a focused positive state.

ANXIETY AND WORRY

Everybody will experience anxiety and worry sometime in their lives. It can occur whenever a person believes something terrible is about to happen now or in the future. The symptoms include trembling, cold sweats, butterflies in the stomach and rapid and shallow breathing.

People will experience anxiety in many different types of situations. It can occur in crowded places, open spaces, work and social gatherings. The most important thing to understand about anxiety is that it is not dangerous and will always pass.

The fears behind anxiety include:

Fear of criticism.
Fear of rejection.
Fear of failure.
Fear of change.
Fear of death.
Fear of fear itself.

In my work as a therapist I have found a frequent cause of anxiety is *performance anxiety.*

This includes public speaking, asking for a pay rise, going for an interview, meeting someone for the first time, and taking an exam. The common attitude that leads to performance anxiety can be summed up in this way: "In this situation whatever terrible thing can go wrong will go wrong and if it does I could not possibly stand it". Dr Albert Ellis has called this catastrophising. People commonly believe that in order to be able to do what they fear they first have to overcome their anxiety. In reality the reverse is true; the key to conquering anxiety is to actually do whatever makes you anxious. Recognise that whatever is worrying you is unlikely to happen and, even if it did, you would probably be able to cope.

Above: anxiety can strike at any time but it is important to know that it is not dangerous and will always pass.

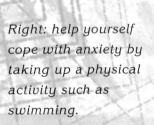

Right: help yourself cope with anxiety by taking up a physical activity such as swimming.

How to cope with anxiety

Remind yourself that feelings of anxiety always pass.
Distract yourself by focusing your attention on someone or something in your surroundings.
Practise relaxation and deep breathing.
Visualise somebody you trust offering you words of encouragement.
Remind yourself that whatever you fear happening is unlikely to happen, and if it does tell yourself that you will find a way to cope.
Take up some physical activity such as brisk walking, running or swimming.

How to cope with worry

Set aside 10 minutes every day to worry. Worry as much as you can for that period of time and then tell yourself that you are not going to worry again till tomorrow.

Think of an amusing scene. For example picture Corporal Jones from the popular television comedy Dad's Army running around shouting "Don't panic! Don't panic!"

Write down what is worrying you. Make a list of all the things you would like to do about the situation. Study this list and then tick all of those items that in reality you can do something about. Act on those – and let go of the others.

PICTURE YOURSELF COPING

Negativity feeds off itself. So if you are always thinking the worst then you may actually talk yourself into more than your fair share of bad experiences. You can use visualisation to cope with a situation that you fear.

This is how it is done:

1. Sit in a comfortable position and close your eyes.

2. Vividly imagine the situation you are anxious about.

3. Feel your anxiety rise.

4. Now picture yourself coping with the situation.

Right: eliminate negative thoughts and feelings by picturing yourself coping with the situation.

5. *Imagine that you are using a breathing technique and talking to yourself in a calm, reassuring way.*

6. *Use coping statements such as: "This is just anxiety; it will soon pass", "I know I will be OK", "This is not as bad as I think".*

7. *When you feel your anxiety decrease, open your eyes.*

Practise the exercise unhurriedly every day for approximately five minutes. If you have a stressful situation coming up, allow as much preparation time as possible. You should start to notice a change in your anxiety after about 30 days.

TAKING CARE OF YOURSELF

The increasing demands of life can make it difficult to take time out and relax. Sometimes people take more care of their cars than they do of their bodies. But a balanced diet, regular exercise, rest and quality sleep will help protect you against stress. Let us look at some of the ways of taking care of yourself so you can lead a healthy and enjoyable life.

THE KEY PRINCIPLES OF HEALTHY EATING

Reduce your intake of fatty foods such as dairy products, fried foods, red meat, sweets and cakes. In place of these, eat lean white meat such as chicken and turkey. Grill and bake your food and steam or boil vegetables. Substitute full-fat milk and butter with semi-skimmed and low-fat spreads. Eat more high-fibre foods such as fresh fruit, wholemeal bread, baked beans and lentils. You can substitute roasted peanuts and crisps with unsalted nuts and dried fruit. Cut down on salt, tea, coffee and sugary drinks as these can affect your mood and cause additional stress.

DRINK ALCOHOL IN MODERATION

Alcohol is high in calories. If you wish to lose weight, you may need to think about reducing the amount of alcohol you consume. Heavy drinking is potentially dangerous and can cause physical and emotional health problems. It can wreak havoc in the family, causing relationships to break down. If alcohol has become a problem, you need to ask yourself why. Do you drink to relax, to gain confidence or to escape from your problems? If the answer to any of these questions is yes, you need to take action and seek professional help.

Left: alcohol should be taken in moderation; if abused it is potentially dangerous, causing both physical and emotional problems.

CHANGE YOUR EATING HABITS

Many people with weight problems have learnt poor eating habits. They may eat at the wrong time, such as in between meals and late at night; some people skip breakfast and lunch; while others use food to satisfy emotional needs, eating when depressed, sad and lonely.

The following tips can help you to change poor eating habits and deal with some of the emotional factors involved.

Eat three times a day, preferably at the same time.

Sit down at the table when eating.

Chew your food slowly as this will aid digestion and stop you from overeating.

If you are trying to lose weight, keep fattening foods out of the house.

Go to the supermarket after you have eaten.

Buy fruit bars instead of sweets and chocolates.

Drink several glasses of water a day as this will fill you up.

Learn to stop eating before you are too full.

Exercise on a regular basis.

If you feel an urge to overeat, ask yourself the following questions:
Am I really hungry now?
If not, am I depressed, lonely, angry or bored?

There is more to losing weight than the latest fad diet. If it were really that simple, you would have lost weight a long time ago. Good food contains the nutrients that protect against disease, but fad

Left: drink several glasses of water a day, it not only fills you up but amazingly helps you to release any retained water in your body.

diets can cause health problems. A healthy, balanced diet and regular exercise will help you to lose weight and keep it off. If you have an eating disorder, it is important that you seek medical advice. Your doctor may suggest that you see a dietician.

What else can I do to deal with my negative emotions other than eat?
Divert yourself into another activity. Practise a relaxation technique, go for a walk, clean your teeth or keep yourself occupied in another way.

Right: regular exercise such as cycling will help you relieve stress as well as improve your health and fitness.

EXERCISE YOUR STRESS AWAY

In times past regular exercise was part of everyday life, as people would often walk long distances to work and for food. But our life styles today are different. We travel by car, sit at our desks all day long and spend time in front of the television. Exercise reduces the risk of heart disease, keeps the body fit and helps reduce stress, anxiety and depression. You do not have to become an Olympic athlete to obtain benefit from exercise. Walking, dancing and swimming are good and pleasurable forms of aerobic exercise that will keep the body fit.

Whenever you exercise it is important to warm up, build the pace up slowly and cool down when you finish.

Exercising three times a week for approximately 20 minutes will usually be sufficient. If you have

health problems or have not exercised for a long time, it is advisable to speak to your doctor before starting.

GIVING UP SMOKING

Most smokers are experts at stopping smoking. They have done it hundreds of times. The skill is to stay stopped and this is a skill that you can learn. If you smoke then stopping needs to be your number one health priority. People can have difficulty accepting the fact that they will experience temporary discomfort while kicking the habit. They may think, "I shouldn't have to experience these terrible feelings of withdrawal", "I can't stand it". When my clients ask for help, one of the first things I will talk about is how natural it is to experience feelings of withdrawal. I then go on to teach them how to cope with these feelings in order to stop smoking permanently.

HOW TO STOP SMOKING

If you *really* want to stop smoking then you need to decide whether you are going to stop *cold turkey* or cut down gradually. In my experience in working with clients by far the best way is to just stop. That way you get the nicotine and other poisons out of your body in the shortest possible time.

If you feel like having a cigarette, repeat one of the following positive coping statements or create some of your own:

Set a date and resolve to stop smoking.

Get a sheet of paper; draw a line down the middle of the page. On the left-hand side, write down all the advantages of becoming a non-smoker, on the right-hand side all the disadvantages of remaining a smoker. If you feel tempted to smoke, read the lists.

A craving for a cigarette will usually last no more than three minutes. If you experience feelings of withdrawal, accept that this is normal and divert yourself with an enjoyable activity.

Change the habits that are associated with your smoking. If you smoke when drinking, try a different type of drink or pick up the glass with the opposite hand. Avoid smoking areas for a few weeks.

Practise relaxation techniques such as progressive relaxation and self-hypnosis.

Even though I feel like a cigarette I can cope without one.

This withdrawal pang will last no more than three minutes. I can stand it.

Use the money you would normally have spent on cigarettes and give yourself a treat.

If you follow this plan, you will soon start to feel healthier. You need to find new ways of relaxing and coping with problems. I have found that sometimes people will rationalise smoking again by thinking, "I wonder if a cigarette still tastes the same? I'll just have one and no more." This is a pitfall you should avoid.

It is very difficult to have just the odd cigarette, so resolve to stay stopped for good.

Below: if you really want to stop smoking then you need to decide whether you are going to stop cold turkey or cut down gradually.

Right: joining an exercise class can encourage you to take regular exercise which in turn will help to solve any sleeping difficulties.

Sleeping problems are very common and there is a lot you can do to help yourself without the need to resort to medication. A restful night's sleep allows the mind and body to repair itself and recharge. Most people seem to need between six and 10 hours' sleep per night. However, as we get older the amount required may reduce. Do not worry if you miss the occasional night's sleep. Even

though you may feel below par, you will usually make up for it the following night.

Sleeping difficulties may be caused by stress experienced during the day. You may be worrying about work or other problems. It is important to use the techniques described in this book to keep worry and anxiety at bay. Relaxation, good eating habits and regular daytime exercise can help.

Right: use your bed for making love and sleep – not for arguments, working or watching television.

How to get a good night's sleep

Make sure your bedroom is not too hot or too cold and that your bed is comfortable.

Go to bed and get up at roughly the same time each day. Sleeping in late is not a good idea as it can make it harder to get to sleep the following night.

Cut down on tea, coffee, alcohol and other stimulants. Replace these with herbal teas and milky drinks.

Use your bed for making love and sleep – not for arguments, working or watching television.

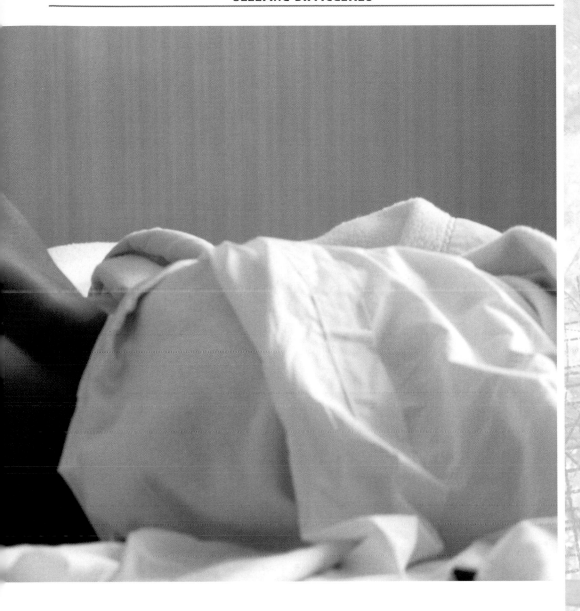

Prepare yourself for bed by having a warm bath and switching off from daytime worries.

When in bed prepare for sleep by practising relaxation and drift off in your imagination to a soothing place.

If you wake up in the night, practice relaxation again.

If you can't get back to sleep, get up and do something boring. When you feel tired, go back to bed.

THE THOUGHT-STOPPING TECHNIQUE

Worries that surface at night can make it difficult to get to sleep. If you find it hard to challenge worrying thoughts that constantly go around in your mind, put an end to them by applying thought-stopping.

The technique involves shouting *Stop!* silently at the thoughts in your mind. Give it some power by imagining it as a voice with real authority. At the same time add an image to the voice, such as a big red stop sign

When the troublesome thoughts are broken, focus on a relaxing image such as a favourite beach or another comfortable place. You can also repeat a relaxing statement to yourself such as, "I can let go of my worries".

Whenever troublesome thoughts return repeat the process.

Thought-stopping will take some time to master as the troubling thoughts often return. Initially it is helpful to learn the technique by shouting *Stop!* out loud at the upsetting thoughts (in the privacy of your own home, of course). Once you have mastered thought-stopping vocally, it will soon become easier to stop the troublesome thoughts silently in your mind.

THERAPIES AND TREATMENTS THAT CAN HELP
YOU TO MANAGE YOUR STRESS

There are many orthodox and complementary therapies that can help you to keep stress at bay. What follows are brief descriptions of some of the most effective.

COGNITIVE BEHAVIOURAL THERAPY

Cognitive behavioural therapy (CBT) is based on the idea that our thoughts affect the way we feel and act towards ourselves, others and the world in general. It is a practical, action-orientated form of therapy in which the therapist and client work together as a team. It is the most extensively researched of all the psychotherapies. CBT can help people with a wide range of problems including stress-management, anxiety and depression. Some of the techniques that have been described in this book come from CBT. Your doctor may be able to refer you to a therapist who practises this form of therapy.

Below: there are many complementary remedies which could help you to keep stress at bay, including a variety of herbal remedies.

CLINICAL HYPNOTHERAPY

Hypnosis is an effective therapy that can help with a wide range of stress- and habit-related problems. Most clients are pleasantly surprised by how natural they feel and certainly how fully aware they are of everything they are experiencing. Hypnosis can provide the key to the subconscious mind and facilitate new ways of dealing with difficulties. There are many doctors, psychologists and therapists that practise clinical hypnotherapy.

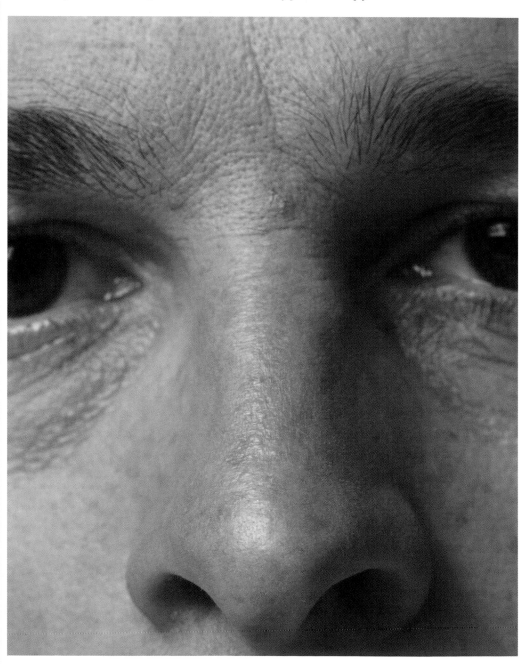

Right: clinical hypnotherapy can be effective treatment for a variety of stress related problems.

Left: aromatherapy provides the perfect way to relax if you have been feeling under stress.

AROMATHERAPY

Aromatherapy dates back several thousand years and was used by ancient civilisations. This therapy is the perfect way to relax if you have been feeling under stress, or as a way of maintaining good health. Essential oils taken from plants are massaged into the body. This soothes tension as well as helping with a wide range of physical, emotional and mental symptoms. Essential oils can also be inhaled and used in the bath.

Right: aromatherapy products come in many forms from candles and incense sticks to essential oils and massage preparations.

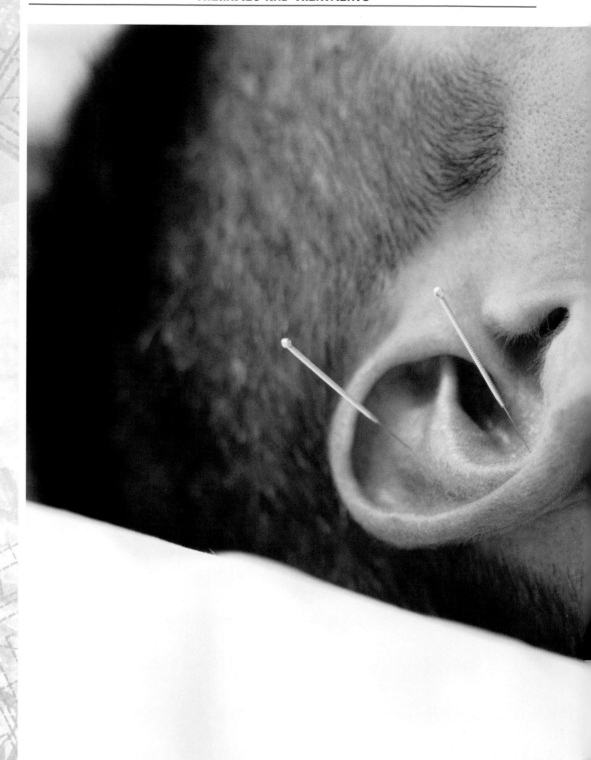

Right: acupuncture can treat a wide variety of conditions including stress, anxiety and depression.

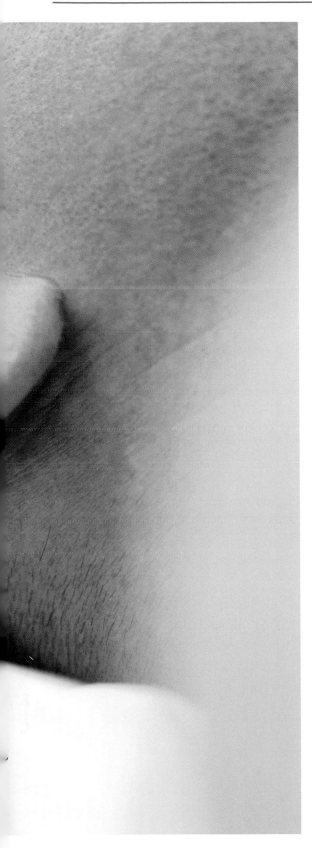

ACUPUNCTURE

Acupuncture restores and maintains health by the stimulation of specific points on the surface of the body. Stainless steel needles are inserted beneath the surface of the skin. The needles are then stimulated by rotation or an electric current. This rectifies the imbalances diagnosed by the acupuncturist. The needles used are very fine so the treatment tends to be painless. Acupuncture can treat a wide variety of conditions including stress, anxiety and depression.

YOGA

The ancient art of yoga is an effective way of developing physical and mental relaxation. There are many schools of yoga. Its ultimate aim is self-enlightenment. However, in the West it is primarily practised for its physical benefits. Yoga consists of physical and mental exercises that help strengthen the body, maintain suppleness and reduce stress.

Right: Yoga consists of physical and mental exercises that help strengthen the body, maintain suppleness and reduce stress.

Left: Homoeopathy is now one of the most popular forms of treatment in the UK.

HOMOEOPATHY

Homoeopathy is a well-established and recognised alternative to conventional medicine. It is now one of the most popular forms of treatment in the UK. The homeopath will ask you about your health in some detail and take a medical history so as to build up an understanding of the causes of your illness. Homeopathic remedies are then given which do not cause side effects.

Homeopathy can help with a wide range of health-related conditions.

IN CONCLUSION

It is sometimes hard to maintain a positive attitude in a world that seems full of obstacles. Negative ideas may cloud our minds and prevent us from getting the most out of life. Contrary to what we might think, our attitude to ourselves and life in general is not set in stone. Hopefully, this book will have shown you effective ways to combat stress. The techniques will work if you work with them, and will enable you to enjoy a healthy, happy and stress-free life. I wish you well.

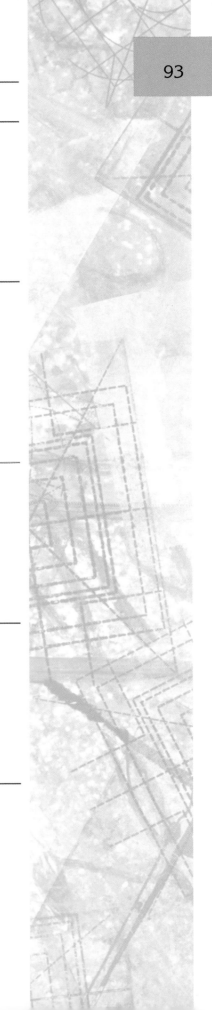

FURTHER READING

FOR THE CHALLENGES OF LIFE

How to cope when the going gets tough

Dr Wendy Dryden and Jack Gordon

Sheldon Press, 1994

Transform yourself!

Ros Taylor

Kogan Page Ltd, 2000

FOR EMOTIONAL MISERY AND DEPRESSION

How to stubbornly refuse to make yourself miserable about anything

– yes anything!

Albert Ellis Ph.D.

Lyle Stuart/Carol Publishing Group, 1996

Overcoming depression

Dr Paul Gilbert

Robinson Publishing Ltd, 1997

FOR SELF-ESTEEM PROBLEMS

10 days to great self-esteem

Dr David Burns

Vermilion, 2000

Hold your head up high

Dr Paul Hauck

Sheldon Press, 1995

FOR ANXIETY AND FEAR

Master your panic and take back your life

Denise F. Beckfield Ph.D.

Impact Publishers, 1998

Healing fear

Edmund Bourne Ph.D.

New Harbinger Publications, Inc, 1998

RELATIONSHIPS AND ASSERTIVENESS

Creating happy relationships

Dr Richard Nelson-Jones

Cassell, 1999

Your perfect right

Robert Alberti Ph.D. and Michael Emmons Ph.D.

Impact Publishers, 1995

INDEX